Advance Praise for
Forging Paths: Beyond Traditional Schooling

If you have ever questioned whether homeschoolers become successful in math, science, engineering, and technology—READ THIS BOOK. If you have a gifted or talented child who finds the school environment oppressive and limiting and you want to find alternatives—READ THIS BOOK. If you already homeschool and would like clear examples of how to create transcripts that earn admission (and scholarships) to some of the most prestigious colleges and universities—READ THIS BOOK. If you want proof that you can modify or skip high school and still get into college and/or have a highly successful career and life—READ THIS BOOK. If you'd like to support your child's passions, enthusiasm for learning, motivation to succeed, and sense of autonomy—READ THIS BOOK. It will help you find an educational path that is truly fulfilling.

— Diane Flynn Keith
   "Your Homeschool Coach and Mentor"
   Editor, Author, Founder, Publisher, www.Homefires.com

If traditional schooling is wilting your child's natural curiosity and genius, read Wes Beach. He shows how homeschoolers, unschoolers, and dissatisfied students everywhere can find radical success with self-directed learning.

— Blake Boles
   Author, *College Without High School*
   Founder, ZeroTuition College

Forging Paths: Beyond Traditional Schooling *brought me close to tears. As a 15-year-old college sophomore, there have been many people along the way who have tried to stop me, including the Early Entry admissions people and several professors. My classmates either think it is really cool, or shun me because before I came along, they were the "smart ones." I know other kids have done what I'm doing, I even know/knew some of them, but I still feel like an abnormality a lot of the time. Reading about these people who have also taken alternative paths, similar to mine, and still found their way in life, I feel closer to them than I do to some of the people that I actually know. It's a really powerful book.*

— Madeline Goodwin
   Former homeschooler, current Southern Oregon University student, future ecologist/biologist

This book reminds readers that there can be alternative paths to success. With the right tools and approach, students and their parents can take charge of their education to accomplish almost anything.
— Shannon Harrison, M.A.
  Young Scholar Program Manager, Family Consultant, and College
  Planning Coordinator at the Davidson Institute for Talent Development

In Forging Paths: Beyond Traditional Schooling, *Wes Beach gives young learners and their families what they so often crave: stories of how education can be different, of how young learners can "take the reins" of their futures.*

From the author's son, who bypassed high school in favor of college and graduate school, to young people who found ways to pursue lives and careers in science, art, and business, with or without college, the stories and voices are what will stay with readers long after closing the final page. Beach also provides experienced and current advice on preparing transcripts for college applications, with specific examples, and getting effective letters of recommendation.

Forging Paths: Beyond Traditional Schooling *is an excellent and inspiring starting point for any family wondering if traditional education may not be the best choice for their child.*
— Lisa Rivero
  Author, *The Smart Teens' Guide to Living with Intensity* and other books on
  education, creativity, and giftedness

Also from GHF Press

*Making the Choice: When Your Typical School
Doesn't Fit Your Atypical Child*

**Look for these Authors
Coming in 2012 from GHF Press**

Jen Merrill
Creator of Laughing at Chaos
http://laughingatchaos.com/

Corin Goodwin and Mika Gustavson
on the topic of
Gifted Homeschooling and Socialization

Forging Paths:
Beyond Traditional Schooling

By Wes Beach

Edited by Sarah J. Wilson

Published by GHF Press
A Division of Gifted Homeschoolers Forum
1257 Siskiyou Blvd. #174
Ashland, OR 97520

ISBN-13: 978-0615577845
ISBN-10: 0615577849

Portions of this book have appeared in altered form in previous publications.

Cover design by Shawn Keehne (skeehne@mac.com).

Dedications

To Leah Udwin for decades of friendship, and for that conversation in 1969 that led to Senior Seminar and all the adventures in education that followed.

And to Judy Hubbard, for love, encouragement, and support, and for our life together.

Contents

Acknowledgments

Three people with the Gifted Homeschoolers Forum had essential roles in the creation of this book. Corin Goodwin repeatedly asked me to write a book, and I finally relented. I don't know where my resistance came from; I loved writing this book. I'm also indebted to Corin for many stimulating conversations over the years. The text I wrote and assembled would not have come into existence in book form were it not for Sarah Wilson's work as editor. Debbie Schwarzer took care of the legal details.

I owe unbounded thanks to the people who allowed me to write about them and who in several cases did a lot of the writing: Brian Beach, Laura Deming, Ciera Kash, Grace Krilanovich, Tierney Logan, Casandra Miller, Theo Paige, Tony Pratkanis, Matthew Snyder, and Jerimi Walker.

A very large number of people, in writing, in conversation, and in practice, have enhanced my view of and work in education. It's impossible to name them all. Thanks go first to the many thousands of students I've worked with during my 50 years in education. They have taught me as least as much as I have taught them. Special thanks go to those who participated in Exploring Advanced Education (EAE) and in Senior Seminar, a small high school program I ran in the late '60s, to be written about in another book. James Herndon never knew it, but for many years I repeatedly returned to his *How to Survive in Your Native*

Land for solace and support. Diane Kaz was instrumental in helping me survive my last years at "Middleroad High School." Jill Boone encouraged me to become involved in the HomeSchool Association of California (HSC) and ultimately to join its board. On that board I met Linda Conrad, who has on several occasions provided the legal help necessary to keep Beach High School alive.

My wife Judy Hubbard stands by me always.

Introduction

This book tells the stories of seven people who took different, nontraditional educational paths and succeeded in a wide variety of ways. Five of these people have experienced varying levels of formal schooling and are not at the time of this writing in school: a computer scientist, an architect, a college math instructor, a restaurant co-owner, and an anti-aging researcher. One person is in a medical residency and another is preparing to begin as a freshman at Stanford. Brief mention is made of other people and their unique paths.

In addition to stories, you'll find discussions of the general principles that made these paths possible and pointers to finding the resources you need to design personalized education for your own kids.

I've indulged in being a memoirist at a few points, so that you understand how I came to be in a position to work with young people outside the system and why I chose to do such work.

I've written about people who spent time as students in my private high school, but I didn't write this book to gain new students. You can design educational pathways on your own. My goal has been to provide empowering information and encouragement.

Beyond finding useful ideas here, and above all else, I hope you will get out from under the weight of a notion that is pervasive in our society, that any highly successful life begins by following a rigidly prescribed path: piling up gold stars in high school—AP courses, a high grade-point average, high test scores—and then matriculating immediately at a prestigious university to complete a degree which can be used as the basis for moving on to graduate or professional school. None of this is necessary. High school can be modified or skipped, or it can be a homeschool; one's path can be meandering; huge amounts can be learned outside of schools. College may not be the best choice; if one does choose college, it need not be an elite college, and admission can be gained, even at elite schools, after very unconventional preparation.

Chapter 1

From No High School to Graduate School

One night when he was eight, I explained to my son Brian at bedtime that we use base 10 numbers, that this means that each place value in numbers increases by a power of 10, and that it's possible to use other bases. This was a brief verbal explanation with no examples or illustrations on paper. This is all I said. The next morning I found him at the breakfast table doing long division in base seven, adding long columns of numbers in base four, and so on. He had worked all this out by himself. His head just works this way. He was in a free school in Ottawa, Ontario, Canada, at this time.

The next year Brian was in an ordinary public school in Portland, Oregon, for the fourth grade. He desperately needed more math than he was getting, so I got him an eighth grade math book, the contents of which he mastered quickly. He spent a lot of time at home, as he was very ill during that year. He complained of lethargy and ran a low-grade fever. Repeated visits to a clinic did not produce a diagnosis.

The following year (1972) our family landed in Santa Cruz County, California (where I've been ever since). I had tried to get my son into an algebra class in a junior or senior high school but had had no success. One principal told me that all parents overestimate their kids, and that was the end of that conversation. Having exhausted every other possibility, I approached a community college math instructor, thinking to hire him as a tutor. He suggested that Brian sit in on his algebra class at the college. I thought to myself that this was a crazy idea, but accepted the offer because nothing else had materialized. Brian went to the five-day-a-week college class three days each week so as not to interrupt each day at his elementary school. He did a very sloppy job on his homework, and I thought we had made a mistake—until he got the second highest score in the class on the final exam.

Brian's illness had disappeared. I became convinced that he had been literally bored sick in Portland.

With special permission from a vice president of the college, Brian audited science and math classes for the next three semesters. Having demonstrated his computing abilities, he was granted full access to the computer center, at that time a large air-conditioned room filled with big machines using punched cards. He was hired by an outside firm as a consultant at age 12.

In the spring before he was due to go to junior high school, we set up an appointment with the school's principal to ask for continued attendance at the community college. This principal, as soon as she understood what we were going to ask for, said, "I hate kids like that." She smiled when she said it, but it didn't matter. We decided that Brian would not attend junior high school.

After another year of auditing, it was time for him to enroll officially at the college. I looked far and wide for support from school officials and even our state senator, and found none. It took me six months to find a way to get Brian enrolled at the college. I found a loophole in the California Education Code (which has since been plugged) that allowed me to convince the principal of the local adult school to give Brian the GED. This principal would not put the results in writing and Brian did not get a certificate, but the principal phoned the results to the college and Brian was admitted as a full-time student.

The rest was easy. Brian completed the transfer admission requirements of the University of California, and then transferred to the University of California, Santa Cruz (UCSC), about 12 miles from home, when he was 14. He was awarded his B.A. in computer science two weeks after his 17th birthday. He had never gone to junior high or high school.

A few years later Brian returned to UCSC and, while working in Silicon Valley, obtained his Ph.D. He is now Vice President and Principal Engineer, Research and Development for TiVo.

Using the Law to Your Advantage

In creating an educational path for Brian, it seemed that there were no existing paths and that there was to be no cooperation or support from school officials. To ensure his well-being, it was necessary to take matters into our own hands and focus on what Brian needed, not on what the schools offered or recommended.

During the time that Brian was auditing classes at Cabrillo College and was not formally enrolled in any school, I considered myself to be his supervising tutor (as opposed to a teaching tutor); I was (and still am) a credentialed teacher. The California Education Code (Section 48224) exempts a student from attending a public school if he is taught by a credentialed tutor three hours per day, 175 days a year, "in the several branches of study required to be taught in the public schools of this state and in the English language. . . . The instruction shall be offered between the hours of 8 o'clock a.m. and 4 o'clock p.m."

I wasn't doing the teaching, but I thought I could argue if necessary that I was indirectly providing instruction by arranging for Brian to audit college classes. I never needed to argue; no one in any official position ever looked into our situation.

You may decide that it's essential to take responsibility for your son's or daughter's education. Laws, regulations, and policies determine what's possible and vary from state to state, province to province, and country to country. I'll provide examples from several U.S. states, but it is beyond the scope of this book to cover the country, let alone the globe. In the United States, a good place to begin to learn about what's legally possible in your state is at Ann Zeise's site, A to Z Home's Cool, at http://homeschooling.gomilpitas.com/index.htm. Start with the "Home School Laws & Legalities" and "Local Home School Support" sections to get an overview of your state's laws and find local groups that can provide you with more information. As you'll see, there is a tremendous amount of information at this site.

Academic Acceleration

Brian's path was a radically accelerated one. Should you consider such a path for your child, you may very well wonder about the wisdom of such an approach, and it's likely that you will encounter the doubts and even the opposition of others.

There is a substantial amount of research to support academic acceleration. Not long after Brian took the first steps on his path, I discovered research that was being done by Julian Stanley and his colleagues at Johns Hopkins. In *Mathematical Talent*, I was reassured to find descriptions of young people who had also jumped ahead in their education and thrived. In *The Academic Acceleration of Gifted Children*, a volume which appeared 17 years after *Mathematical Talent*, Stanley and Linda Brody wrote that research shows that kids who enter college early are successful in their studies and in subsequent endeavors, and that they do not encounter significant social or emotional difficulties. The preponderance of more recent research confirms this.

Accessing Community College

Beginning an educational path like Brian's requires finding ways into a community college. Many young people may choose to start with classes at a community college while still homeschooling. While I'll discuss this option in Chapter 5, here the focus is on regular admission.

In many states, people are admitted as regular students to community colleges if they have a high school diploma or its equivalent. This is true in California for people younger than 18 (anyone 18 or older is accepted at community college with or without a diploma). Parents who are homeschooling independently after setting up their own private high school can issue a diploma to and write a transcript for their kid at any time, on any basis whatsoever. California law sets no requirements of any kind for graduation from a private high school. Alternatively, an equivalent certificate can be earned by passing the California High School Proficiency Examination (CHSPE). Anyone 16 or older can take this test. Also, parents who are homeschooling independently can, whenever they believe it's appropriate to do so, advance their child to a grade that makes her eligible to take this exam.

Other states provide different admission possibilities. You may find the key in your state's laws, which you may be able to search on the Internet. For example, Title 15, Section 15-1821(A) of the Arizona revised statues states, "Each community college district board shall adopt policies which require community colleges under its jurisdiction to admit students under age eighteen who have not yet attained a high school diploma or high school certificate of equivalency and who meet the established requirements of the courses for which they enroll." And 15-1821(B)(1) states, "No student under age eighteen shall be denied admission because of age, lack of a high school diploma or high school certificate of equivalency, grade in school, lack of permission of school officials or lack of concurrent enrollment in a public or private school, if the student has achieved at least a specified score on a college entrance examination." [1]

In Virginia, Tidewater Community College's special admissions policy says that young people who are homeschooled can apply as exceptions. Such students must show that they have complied with Virginia's homeschooling regulations and obtain specified evidence that they are working at grade level. [2]

A certificate earned through the GED will provide admission to a community college. In some states it's possible to take the GED at 16. You can find out about this possibility in your state by entering "GED age waiver [your state]" in your preferred search engine.

Make It Happen

Regardless of the state you live in, if you investigate carefully, dig deep enough, and persist in seeking information, you may be able to provide for community college admission for your son or daughter who has not completed or even begun a traditional high school education. Read college websites, talk to college officials, listen to other homeschoolers, read your state's education laws. You will probably have to sift through conflicting advice and opinions. Don't rule out the possibility of special permission from a college's administrators or the board. Don't give up until you've exhausted all possibilities.

Once your child is in a community college, moving on to almost any four-year college or university will be based only on his community college record. For example, the University of Oregon considers only one's college record if 36 quarter (or 24 semester) units have been completed along with one college-level composition course and one college-level mathematics course, and if second-language proficiency can be demonstrated. [3]

Beginning at a community college after a shortened or non-existent stay in high school is one creative path for eager and bright students. In the following chapters, I'll present paths that include nontraditional ways of completing high school, direct and delayed admission to four-year colleges and universities, stopping out of college, and gaining a post-secondary education in the "real world" instead of college.

Chapter 2

A Short Stay in Public High School Leads to Graduate School, Eventually

When Brian graduated from the University of California, Santa Cruz, I had been teaching science and math for ten years at a public high school I'll call Middleroad (MHS). The previous year I had also set up a small program in the district for gifted students. A major change in California's gifted education policy provided me with an opportunity to initiate a larger program at Middleroad High School; the principal named the program Exploring Advanced Education (EAE). At the outset I wasn't entirely clear what I wanted to accomplish with this program, and, while I often lay awake at night during the summer before the program started, I worried about how whatever I did might disrupt students' lives.

When the fall semester began, I met 22 students in a class period set aside for EAE, and we began talking about how they experienced school. What quickly evolved was an exploration of educational options, and then a menu of options available to EAE students. People in EAE could:

- with their permanent hall passes move about the school more freely than other students
- devise courses which they pursued individually and independently

- challenge existing courses, earning credit for them by examination
- enroll in distance learning courses
- enroll concurrently in high school and community college classes
- take all their classes at the local community college (by special arrangement with the college)
- earn a high-school-diploma-equivalent certificate by passing the California High School Proficiency Examination (CHSPE) and leave high school early (an option open to all eligible high school students throughout California)

Matthew's Journey Begins

Matthew Snyder joined EAE when he came to Middleroad, where he says he had a "rather typical first year at high school." (Matthew has provided me with 12 pages of rich prose describing his educational history; I can only quote limited pieces of it here.) He chose to take all his sophomore-year classes at the local community college. Toward the end of this year he took and passed the CHSPE.

"Once I passed the CHSPE, my relationship to any high school was complete. The threads that tie my following education together have mostly to do with exploring ways of making things. I borrowed and made tools and made things at home." These things were many and varied, and included polished oak finger rings, skateboard ramps, and a rebuilt Porsche. "I made houses, working with the contractors who built our family house when we first moved to Santa Cruz Mountains, and later for a series of contractors, starting with a good friend's father." Matthew took musical instruments apart and rebuilt them, wrote stories, explored photography, and learned computer programming, desktop publishing, and technical drawing.

De Anza College, a community college in another county, was known to prepare students well for transferring to the University of California, Berkeley. Thinking he would transfer to UC Berkeley and study engineering, Matthew took up studies at De Anza, focusing on engineering and music. "Starting De Anza, I finished rebuilding the antique Porsche, and commuted from Santa Cruz, while at the same time accumulating carpenter's tools and working, sometimes full time, as a carpenter on various residential and light commercial projects in Santa Cruz County, sometimes finding projects on my own, drawing, designing, and building decks or home remodels and additions, sometimes working for one of two building contractors. I was about 16 or 17 years old."

Matthew, tired of "institutional processes" and commuting, wondered if engineering would lead to a "cubicle job," and thought of his sister's trip to Latin America. "Sometime in the middle of my fourth semester at De Anza, I dropped out and planned a trip to Mexico."

Bends in the Path

Traveling in Mexico with a friend, he met some people from Colorado whose talk of the mountains was enough to prompt him to head back to the U.S. and settle in Park City, Utah, where he stayed for two years, living the life of a ski bum, "[i]ntentionally leaving my construction tools behind, because the mountains seemed just too cold to work as a carpenter, I worked at the weekly paper, in charge of the newspaper darkroom, skied, and began some intense work in both color and black and white photography."

"After a time it felt to me I needed to return to 'real life' (or, perhaps, to discover what 'real life' was)." Matthew moved to Los Angeles and worked as a full-time carpenter. He worked "on several small scale, but key, architectural projects. With my new tools and new skills, I made furniture, selling some in a gallery/showroom in Santa Monica. I made more photographs, teaching myself how to use a large format camera and print contact prints in a closet like Edward Weston did. And I wanted to read Shakespeare and write."

Matthew entered California State University, Long Beach, and earned a degree in creative writing. He then moved to San Francisco, where he worked for two firms and "made time to design a high rise building and create a portfolio of drawings and renderings." He was creating his admissions portfolio for architecture grad school and describes his creative process this way:

"Applying to grad school appeared to be the testing ground for well-crafted creative writing and good design. It seemed to me that there were many characteristics of myself and my life that would be unattractive to a grad school admissions committee, but that there would be a few that they would find favorable. It was a matter of creating an admissions package which would create a persona that would be admitted.

"The process felt very much like any creative work. There were six components: GPA, GRE, portfolio, letters of recommendation, personal essay, CV. I received much advice about the process, read a number of excellent books on applications and entrance essays, selected my top schools and my safe schools, traveled to a number of them, met with deans and architecture professors and asked them to review my portfolio and offer any recommendations for my application.

'The short story is I applied to Harvard, Columbia, Rhode Island School of Design, Southern California Institute of Architecture, and the University of California, Berkeley. I was admitted to every school with varying degrees of scholarship funding, selected Harvard, received further tuition scholarship assistance after my first year there, and graduated second in my class."

In Boston, Matthew became a partner in a "small, academic-design-oriented firm" and "taught several design studios at the Northeastern University School of Architecture." He now lives in Santa Cruz. "I travel to Boston or other project locations for a week each month, and spend a number of hours on Skype or the telephone." Again, in his words:

"There are still many ways I suspect I will respond to and participate with this profession that are non-institutionalized and non-standard. The key value I sought from Harvard was credibility, and a credential that will give me a small amount of support when I choose to do something that was never done before. However, rather than follow any established path, what guided me was a series of decisions to follow and do those things that seemed to be deeply important to me. There have been many moments where I felt a huge amount of guilt for the apparent disregard to the standards which those around me were following, and it has raised eyebrows and the occasional comment that what I was doing was not acceptable. Yet focusing on the work, making objects, making architecture, understanding graphic design and typography, dipping into movie making, screenwriting, video editing, deeply understanding film photography and then digital photography, learning how to make digital 3D models and render them, and how to make drawings with paper, pen, and pencil, and then with digital CAD tools, learning poetry and fiction how to read it and how to make it, learning musical theory and performance, has kept opportunities coming, and allowed me to work at a very high level rather than following someone else's instructions. What happened over the now thirty years of this experiment is that the whirling storm of digital technology centered in the Silicon Valley where I have done much work, has unified nearly all forms of designing and making, and now nearly every tool I use in photography, music, video, 3D modeling, graphic design works on a similar digital platform in an unexpected and seamless workflow. Creating a building from the imagination and rendering it or photographing one already built and editing and adjusting the photographs are very similar tasks, and architecture has settled out as the unique practice that captures the intersection of each of these threads.

"The remaining piece is that of fiction, and will be my most important project in the weeks and months to come, as my 'day job' continues to be centered on architecture. The writing that I began twenty years ago had promising qualities at the local scale, but lacked structure necessary to contain a larger work. Interestingly, it was an education in architecture that taught me how to handle structure at a range of scales from the fastener to the metropolitan, and has given me the tools to realize the fiction I began to imagine making over thirty years ago."

The Grand GITMOR

An often-repeated, widely-believed notion is that to be very successful in today's world, it's essential to complete high school with a record showing many AP courses, a very high grade point average, high SAT or ACT scores, and deep involvement in extracurricular or outside activities, and then go on straight through college and graduate school. Matthew's story clearly demonstrates this path is not necessary and can be dramatically modified with impunity. Nothing he did in his short stay in high school had anything to do with his acceptance at Cabrillo College, De Anza College, California State University, or Harvard. The GRE was his "first standardized test since taking Iowa Tests in grade school in the 1970s." He obviously did not go straight through school. And what he learned and accomplished during the times he stopped out was important in gaining admission to Harvard. Matthew's path has been "non-standard" and in large measure "non-institutionalized," and it has led to many achievements, successes, and much fulfillment.

The Grand GITMOR (Guide for Independent and Tough-Minded Owners of Responsibility) was posted on the EAE classroom wall: "Your Education Is Your Responsibility." I took this seriously and did not prescribe any educational path for anyone. But, believing that one of the negative aspects of high school was the compulsion to be there, I did urge everyone to take the CHSPE so that they would know that they could leave high school at any time. State policy allowed (and still does allow) people who have earned a certificate earned through the CHSPE to remain in high school if they so chose. What I told EAE participants was that if they had a certificate and chose to stay in high school, they could wake up every morning and know that they were going to school because they chose to do so, not because state law compelled them.

A number of people who passed the CHSPE did choose to leave high school early. Several years into EAE I decided to track down the first nine early leavers and see how they had fared. Every one of them had earned a BA, and several were in or on their way to graduate school. Although I do not believe that college is right for everyone, the school did. So these accelerated students had all succeeded on the school's terms. But even this information about students' successes did not impress school officials. Their attitude seemed to be, "What you describe didn't happen, and even if it did, so what?" My sense was that the school wanted to call the shots, and since these students took their education into their own hands and did not follow the traditional four-years-in-high-school route dictated by the school, nothing they did was significant.

Some of the first students in EAE tried to challenge the drivers' education course at Middleroad, and did not like that the instructor insisted on a series of quizzes followed by an exam rather than the single exam mentioned in the school's policy on challenging courses. California law allows individuals to easily set up a private school, so my response to this situation was to set up my own private high school, Beach High School (BHS), and offer EAE students an opportunity to enroll in BHS concurrently and take drivers' education in their second school.

As it turned out, a number of other things could be accomplished in a similar way, and it became routine for EAE students to enroll in BHS while continuing to attend Middleroad. Eventually one student (who is now a veterinarian), and then others, left MHS to enroll in my school so they could pursue their learning paths on their terms. At this point I decided I could do the work I valued much more effectively on my own, so I resigned from MHS.

Chapter 3

Autodidact Finds a Way to Soar

I first set up Beach High School in 1981 in connection with EAE (Exploring Advanced Education), my gifted program at Middleroad High School, and began working full time through it after resigning from MHS in 1993. My school serves young people who do not believe that a traditional high school education is what they want or need. My students often graduate shortly after enrolling, sometimes at 16 or 15 or 14, occasionally even earlier, on the basis of their readiness to move on with their lives, as well as their maturity and personal strengths, all which are documented on a BHS transcript. Others stay enrolled for months or years, engaging in endeavors of their choice. They, too, graduate with a diploma and a transcript showing their achievements. These people succeed in wonderful ways, including academically in college, because they make deliberate, informed, and deeply personal decisions to move on. They have accomplished a great deal in practical crafts, the arts, business, and the professions, and often reach the highest levels of formal education. Their successes do not depend on completion of academic coursework at the high school level. Instead, their recognition of their genuine interests and talents and their self-knowledge, confidence, enthusiasm, determination, ability to persevere, and sense of autonomy carry them where they want to go.

Jerimi Walker's Story

Jerimi Walker contacted me early in 1997. She had, after teaching herself a substantial amount of math as a homeschooler, enrolled in a public high school. She had asked to be placed in an advanced class, but school officials discounted her self-teaching and placed her first in a beginning algebra class, then in geometry, finally in second-year algebra. Frustrated, Jerimi was looking for a way to study at the level she was prepared for. After some discussion through e-mail (Jerimi was in Alabama), we decided she might succeed in gaining admission to Troy University, the state school in her hometown.

Jerimi had taken an online class in holography, made her own laser, and sent me a hologram she had made. This was a clear indication of her success as an autodidact and convinced me that I could take her statements about what else she had learned at face value. Her BHS transcript shows four courses completed at the public high school and an untraditional mix of 20 self-taught courses including Holography 1 and 2, Lasers and Applications, Meteorology, Basic Electronics, and Small Business Origination and Management. This transcript also includes narrative material, written by Jerimi; the instructor of her holography course, who was at Lehigh University; and a retired high school physics and chemistry teacher and a long-time community college part-time chemistry and physics instructor, whom she had met online.

Because BHS is unaccredited, Jerimi's application went to a special admissions committee at Troy University. After some discussion with them and revisions to Jerimi's transcript, she was admitted. Her story continues in her own words (reproduced with the permission of Jerimi Walker and the Gifted Homeschoolers Forum, from the April 2011 issue of *A Word from GHF*):

"My homeschooling journey was an extremely positive experience and has defined a large part of my life in the years since. We homeschooled with little structure and one goal: to have fun exploring and learning. Studying meteorology didn't just involve learning why things happened but seeing it first hand by driving around after a large hurricane. Learning about physics involved making holograms, and we all (my brother, sister, and I) learned about computers by building small websites through hand-coded HTML (this was the mid 90s, to keep the technology in perspective). We even tried starting a small business for a while that was based on the holograms, which taught me a great deal about a variety of topics.

"Eventually, I became very focused on going out into the world as an adult and saw college as a key part in this plan. Attending a local college, I worked hard taking extra classes and was able to graduate with my bachelor's degree in mathematics when I was 17. As I saw it, this was the first step in my master plan!

"I immediately enrolled in a math Ph.D. program at Syracuse University, but within a couple of years felt that I was missing out on something that I couldn't quite put my finger on. I ended up leaving the program and worked different jobs, even playing in band. While at the time there was this feeling of 'quitting,' in retrospect it was really important to simply get some perspective outside of academia.

"I did eventually return to graduate school, opting to go for my masters in applied math through the University of Minnesota Duluth. This really was a great time, and while taking classes I had the chance to try my hand at entrepreneurship again by starting the Air Career and Gear Expo, which was designed to connect young people interested in flight with schools and other programs. It was reasonably successful and I met a bunch of great people through the process.

"After graduating, I was determined to find a job which allowed me to talk about math as much as I wanted, while providing a work/life balance. I was lucky enough to find a perfect fit and am now a college math instructor.

"It is my belief that this meandering path is exactly what life is all about and it is easy to see how much of a role homeschooling played in shaping this. Each day is about learning and experiences. Without my homeschooling experience, I may have never had the guts to go to college and then later to leave graduate school. All of this is part of who I am today. I am now close to thirty years old and will continue to try new things and have the same love for learning that I had years ago as a homeschooler. I have no idea where it will eventually take me. That's the fun part!"

Jerimi recently started an online math website called Math Bootcamps, designed to fill in the gaps left by high school and college courses.

Unfounded Concerns

One of my concerns was that Jerimi would have difficulty getting into a highly regarded graduate school after earning her bachelors at a little-known state school. But, as her story explains, she was admitted to Syracuse. What she didn't mention is that she was awarded a full scholarship.

Jerimi is now a math professor at a community college outside of Chicago.

I've written a number of transcripts for homeschooled, self-taught people, and these transcripts, from my unaccredited school that consists of nothing more than a home office and an attitude, have accompanied successful applications to Stanford, Caltech, MIT, Rice, University of California at Berkeley, NYU, Washington University in St. Louis, the Rhode Island School of Design, and many other schools. I may have experience beyond most homeschooling families, but such families can create home-grown transcripts that are just as effective as mine. I'll discuss writing transcripts in Chapter 9.

Chapter 4

"Real World" Success Without College

Here in the middle of stories about people who went to college is the story of a woman who decided to become an unschooler after high school and has pursued a post-secondary education outside of academia. Even if your child has made a firm decision to go to college, encourage her to back it up and confirm it by considering the possibility of not going.

Dale Stephens, like Laura Deming (see Chapter 6), is a Thiel Fellow. His project is to develop resources to support people who choose to skip or modify formal higher education. He has created a website (www.uncollege.org) and is writing a book. At the website you will find thought-provoking reading material, exercises, and images.

Unschooler after High-Schooler:

One evening at a Santa Cruz restaurant we often go to, my wife and I chatted with our waitperson, and then with another staff person who came by. She said something to us about choosing not to go to college. Always interested in hearing educational histories, I asked if I could come back to learn more. She agreed. The next day I learned that her name is Ciera Kash, and she told me about her adventurous life.

During a subsequent conversation over breakfast, she agreed to put her story in writing.

Ciera Kash's Story

"My parents put me in gymnastics at the age of five. I was naturally petite and off the wall; the sport channeled my high energy and put it to good use. I don't remember much besides my time traveling, competing, and training with my team from the ages of five to fifteen because I spent so many hours in the gym—year-round, weekends, five-hour practices after school. It is said that when somebody is highly involved in something that mentally and physically dominates your life, the brain filters out everything else. (My few vivid memories included skiing with my dad and brother since I was five years old and singing with my dad as he played guitar when my brother and I brushed our teeth and got ready for bed. Snow sports, water sports, and music were always a large part of my life.) I ended up competing with a team called Airborne Gymnastics where only the very serious trained. Gymnastics is special in that it is an individual sport and a team sport. Every day consisted of vigorous conditioning and repetitive training. To say the least, there was a lot of crying and a lot of pressure, but we all had each other. What started out as a true passion and desire to go the Olympics became a love/hate relationship with the sport. I was so nervous competing all those years, but the feeling I would get after winning was like nothing else, a natural high that most athletes can identify with and become addicted to.

"It is my belief that you can be good at anything if you just abandon your initial fears which, if you think about it, are in your control. It is all about understanding what you love and strengthening your ability to overcome fear and channeling your energy into it completely. Of course, everybody needs some sort of positive influence to help them excel and push through. My coach at Airborne Gymnastics was a very tough man. But for some reason he made me want to prove something to him. He would remind me once in a while that I had true talent and physical strength, so I yearned to live up to his expectations. Nothing good comes easily, I realize now. If something were easy, everybody would be doing it. My father always told me that as long as you're learning and are persistent, that's all that matters. Everybody is good at something; they just have to persevere.

"The last year I spent at Airborne Gymnastics was forced, partly by the loyalty I felt towards my teammates, partly by my coaches, and partly by my parents. I stuck it out until eighth grade when I felt like I was missing out on life. It was the point when I knew I wanted to quit 100%. I was truly done and ready to move on. The 30-minute drive to the gym that day was sickening. I was so nervous we had to pull over so I could throw up.

"I have never regretted quitting, because the decision was not irrational and I was absolutely ready and excited for the rest of my life.

"I have known a lot of people who had a hard time focusing in school. Every one of them had something else they had true passion for. Whether it was music, art, skateboarding, or dancing, it was those things that drew me to those who would become my friends. I think I was drawn to these people because I, too, was not passionate about the things I was learning in school; I was fascinated by music, art, counter-culture sports, and philosophy.

"In particular I had a friend named Nikki that I met freshman year in high school who introduced me to guitar playing and art. I had another friend, Ali, who did horribly in school but was the most amazing dancer you've ever seen.

"Nikki, Ali, and I took a Christmas trip to Tahoe where we went snowboarding. Ali's sister's boyfriend was already an incredible rider and watched me hit jumps after two weeks and get good really fast. I attribute this to gymnastics, because to me, nothing could be more difficult and painful than gymnastics. He took me through the park and kept telling me how impressed he was. I wanted to keep up, so I pushed myself to do everything he could do. After that trip, he was adamant that I was a natural and should pursue it professionally. When

I got my drivers permit I made my dad let me drive up to Tahoe in snow storms so he would trust me to do it as soon as I got my drivers license. At 16, I was driving myself up to Tahoe and staying at my grandparents' house almost every weekend, sometimes with friends, but mostly just by myself because I was completely obsessed.

"I got extremely good grades in high school because the rule was that if I did well in school, I had all the freedom and trust in the world from my parents. I took Honors English, Art History, and Art because those subjects always did interest me and came naturally; the teachers gave me positive encouragement. Junior year came around and all of a sudden it was all about where you would be going to college. People in the town of Los Altos had a lot of money and could afford to send their kids to college. College was not a privilege but an expectation. I visited my older brother at UC Davis and other friends at their colleges and what I saw blew me away—drinking, drugs, and basically a free four-year party.

"The conversations of the overindulged all centered on 'What college are you going to?' and 'Where are you applying?' I got very turned off of the whole idea of Los Altos kids being entitled to go to college. I saw various kids who had finished college who were just as lost as before they entered, without work and a work ethic. I felt like there was more potential for me in snowboarding than sitting in a classroom spending my parents' money. I had much too much energy to go to school for another four years without direction. I knew what I wanted and school wasn't going to get me there

"I think parents discount their children's ability to know what they love and trust in their feelings towards certain things. I feel like people know what they're good at and what they're not at an early age. Teachers and schooling let us know through grading, and naturally we thrive on being good at something and being acknowledged for it.

"After high school I wanted to live in Whistler/Blackcomb, British Columbia, so I could train seriously and eventually begin competing. I went there with my mom to find a room to rent so that when I got back from my planned summer training in New Zealand, I would be ready to settle into BC.

"So I went to a snowboard training school to New Zealand since it was their winter. I worked really hard and learned a lot. Among other things, we learned how to drop out of helicopters and free ride in the deep powder. One of my friends had to get airlifted out, she got so injured. I stayed an additional month after the camp in a hostel by myself with an extremely diverse group of people, all snowboarding. I hitchhiked up to the mountain every morning.

"I got to BC and moved into this house with four stories and six rooms. The deal with my family was that if I wasn't going to go to college, then I had to get a job and support myself. I had a couple of months to find a job and save up enough money before winter came. I figured out that one must have a work visa to get a job, so I tried and tried but was told I couldn't get one. I guess they didn't want Americans to take their jobs.

"I then decided I would move to Tahoe where I grew up snowboarding and figured I could still do what I needed to do there, as well as find a job to support myself. I got a job at Northstar at Tahoe as a demo-technician where I tuned skis and boards and assisted customers in understanding the differences among the newest skis and boards that they could try out and potentially buy. I had a second job at Java Hut, the local Kings Beach coffee house.

"I blew out my knee that year and so I had to leave my jobs and snowboarding for the winter. I did a lot of physical therapy, and my mom and then-boyfriend helped me to recover. I lived with my boyfriend in Santa Cruz that summer. When I went back to Tahoe for the winter I had an awesome full winter training there. I was against joining a training team with a coach because snowboarding was something I could learn from the friends (mostly men who were professionals) I met who pushed me to get better. That summer I traveled to Costa Rica to surf. When I came back, I lived in a friend's house in Pescadero and got a job at Johnny's Harborside Restaurant at the Santa Cruz Harbor as a busser; my dad knew the owner, and so helped me get the job. That was my introduction to Johnny's! I found an old friend surfing one day up north of Santa Cruz and he had a room for rent in the Seabright area in Santa Cruz. With my dog I moved in with the people there, half working people, half college students. I loved biking to work and surfing.

"I knew I just had to keep learning, so come winter I moved back up to Tahoe to train. I went back to Tahoe and worked at CB's Pizza as a server as well as at Alpine Ski Resort as a snowboard instructor. That next winter, I blew out my knee again early in the season. I had my MCL (medial collateral ligament) taken out and my hamstring tendon grafted onto my ACL (anterior cruciate ligament). I lost my two jobs because I couldn't walk, so I worked on recovering.

"During the down time, I bought Adobe Photoshop and worked on designing snowboard art. I created a portfolio and hooked up with a small local snowboard company out of Reno called Sentury Snowboards. I ended up designing a couple of snowboards for them, but made little money doing it. My friend offered me a quick job in Las Vegas painting for her mother's faux finishing company. We drove there and worked for three weeks on a job that made me some really good money. I thoroughly enjoyed it, working with my hands, and realized it was a good way to make money doing something I loved in the meantime. When I got back from Vegas, I immediately began plastering for work. I got a big job in Colorado, a bunch of jobs in Los Altos Hills; it was steady for some time. Eventually, work just slowed down. I then got a part-time job at a bakery in Campbell and got so consumed with it, that the plastering jobs just kind of got put on hold.

"I was working, but not enough and a little bored with my life, when my dad called me one day with some news. He told me the owners of Johnny's were having issues and wanted to sell the business and return to my dad the money he had invested—unless we wanted to take it over and get involved. I told him I would mull it over. Becoming quite the foodie and always having trouble saying no to opportunities, I said I would give it a try. The following week I went in to meet one of the owners, who was going to teach me everything I needed to know. I was told I was just going to be doing administrative work, 10-20 hours a week. But once I was in, there was no turning back. It was a tough road working under somebody who seemed to know it all, but I wouldn't let myself fail. I became manager and was putting in 50 hours a week on average. It was the only way to get the business running properly. The first eight months were excessively challenging to me because I am naturally more of an artist/maker than a manager. I had to force myself to confront people and be a leader. I decided the best way to lead is to show everyone that I was dedicated and qualified. I learned every aspect of the front of the house and worked with my staff day after day. I learned how to budget, schedule, advertise, host events, work on seasonal menu changes, run staff meetings, gain wine knowledge, manage bartender pouring, hire staff, fix things that seem to break every day, and so on.

"Today, the restaurant is my life and I made a promise to myself to stick it out for at least two years. I am going on a year and a half and I can't even imagine saying goodbye. Johnny's has become a huge part of my life and I basically live it every day. It is the most challenging and rewarding line of work I have ever experienced. The familiar faces, progressive teamwork, and amazing food keep me doing it. We've finally found a chef that is in for the long haul and the other owners have potential plans to build a deck and expand the business even more. I am not sure this is something I want, but we will see what happens. Since joining the team, I have seen the morale and financials turn for the better. I will continue to do my best to keep Johnny's an inviting place with extraordinary fresh food/seafood from the harbor. I am trying to manage my life, while finding time to surf and be with my boyfriend, dog, and family. It is a never-ending balancing act. I would like to be able to buy some land by the ocean in these hard times, so all I can do is keep it up and be PERSISTENT. I think that's the name of the game."

Passion and Persistence

High school studies are claimed to be absolutely necessary preparation for life, whether one chooses to go to college or not. But I don't believe Ciera's high school studies were essential for her to succeed in her many post-high-school endeavors. She wrote in an e-mail, "I treated school like it was work, just a job, something that I did because I had to in order to be taken seriously by my parents. That way I could partake in my true passions, as well." It's the passions that matter, and it's the persistence that she mentions. It's also the resourcefulness, self-reliance, and high degree of motivation that her story clearly demonstrates.

The nearly 1,400 graduates of Beach High School help make the case for the primacy of personal traits in success. They have bypassed much or all of the supposedly essential preparation that high school provides, and they have succeeded in a wide variety of vocations, ranging from medicine and law to professional rock climbing and dance. And, although they have turned their back on formal education at the secondary level, many of them have become college professors. Foundational in their achievements are their recognition of their genuine interests and talents and their self-knowledge, confidence, enthusiasm, determination, ability to persevere, and sense of autonomy.

Chapter 5

Straight from Homeschool to University

Tony Pratkanis's Parents Decide to Homeschool

"Our decision to homeschool Tony was made only after exhausting all of the traditional options available in our geographic location. Neither of us had ever contemplated homeschooling until we found that we were unable to meet Tony's educational needs with the local schools. Tony had an innate love of learning that we worked extremely hard to nurture. He learned best through exploration and project-based learning approaches. Moreover, his overriding interests centered heavily on science and technology. We were not satisfied that the local options would meet either of those needs. A homeschool approach allowed us to capitalize on those interests and to continue to reinforce his very strong desire to find out how the world works, to question why things are the way they are, and to find new and creative ways of doing things.

"Tony went to a private school for kindergarten and for three months of first grade. After that, he was enrolled in an independent study program in the school district. We found that program to be outstanding. We met with a teacher every two weeks to review our progress, discuss Tony's educational needs, and identify new resources to keep him challenged. Those sessions were incredibly helpful. The teacher had a terrific command of all disciplines and was extremely good at diagnosing Tony's interests, learning style, and capabilities. The program offered 'class' sessions on specific topics (such as computer programming, biology, etc.) that allowed the children to experience group learning settings. Field trips were also an important resource as these provided opportunities for hands-on learning and for socialization experiences. At the same time, Tony was also enrolled in Stanford University's Education Program for Gifted Youth (EPGY), through which he completed mathematics, science, and computer science courses."

The High School Transcript

Upon completing the independent study program, Tony enrolled at BHS when he was 14 and remained my student for five years (he delayed college applications for a year due to a health issue). He completed math, science, and computer programming classes at a community college and through EPGY, and he independently engaged in high-level study and work. BHS provided a way for Tony to be legally enrolled in a school while he homeschooled. I assisted in developing a homeschooling strategy and content and provided the paperwork necessary for him to enroll in classes at a community college as a high school student. When he was ready to apply to four-year colleges, I wrote a transcript and the Secondary School Report that went to the colleges Tony applied to; the report included the following recommendation describing his learning experiences while at BHS.

I am delighted to write a letter of recommendation for Anthony Turner Pratkanis in support of his application to Stanford [or other] University. Tony is in his senior year of high school, where he has completed a rigorous course of study, particularly in the science and mathematics areas. His course work (including 15 community college courses) has been specifically designed to take advantage of his strengths and passionate interests in computer science, robotics, and chemistry. He

28

will graduate from Beach High School, where I am the director, in June of 2011 with a GPA very close to his present 4.76.

For the last three years, Tony has had a very unique and wonderful educational experience working as a software intern for Willow Garage. (He will continue his involvement with Willow Garage through the summer of 2011). Willow Garage is a start-up robotics company creating open source software such as ROS and Open-CV and has developed a research robot called PR-2, several of which have been donated to universities. While at Willow Garage, Tony has contributed to the library of open source software and developed his skills in such areas as indoor navigation with A*-based planners, indoor mapping with SLAM, deliberative action planner (Teleo-Reactive Executive – T-REX), and automated testing for a telepresence robot (Texai). He was also fortunate enough to participate in a T-REX project that resulted in a conference paper, on which he is a co-author, and he gave a company-wide talk about his work.

For his first two internships, Tony worked on the team that developed T-REX (a planning algorithm). This team consisted of a team leader plus two to three graduate student interns and Tony. In the second internship, this team worked with a team from NASA-Ames on shared code between T-REX and the NASA version. This required Tony to work with two sets of team members (often with diverse goals) to establish a direction for programming code development. In his third year, Tony was invited to join an intact team commercializing a telepresence robot called Texai. He was invited to join the team because of his ability to debug code and for his teamwork abilities. In this setting, Tony learned to negotiate with team members, communicate objectives, make presentations, and listen to others. Tony has also developed both his technical skills and his social skills in a variety of other settings. From a young age, he was a member of the Swanton Pacific Railroad Society (a group that maintains historically-significant 1/3-size steam locomotives). In this society, Tony worked in teams to do such tasks as lay track, pour cement, assemble trains, perform electrical work, among other tasks. Indeed, it was at the Swanton Pacific that he learned his teamwork skills. Similarly, his membership in the Homebrew Robotics Club (HBRC) allowed him to develop numerous technical and professional skills while simultaneously providing him with the opportunity to enhance his social skills. As a member of the HBRC, he worked with others to build robots, made presentations to large audiences, and competed in contests, learning how to both win and lose gracefully. Tony was fortunate to be invited to be a mentor in a pilot program by Maker Faire (a project of O'Reilly Media) to link mentors with young, new makers and creators (in this case, Tony mentored a middle-schooler in developing a telepresence robot). He has also worked as a volunteer judge (on software development) for the CalGames (associated with the FIRST robotics program) To develop his communication skills, he has presented his robots in various mass media formats, including CBS Sunday Morning and Click, the BBC Tech Program. His written communication skills were enhanced by co-authoring an article about his robot for Servo magazine. He has been a volunteer at the California Academy of Science where he also worked as an intern on ants.

As you can see on Tony's transcript, he has taken an extensive amount of courses with many of them coming at the college level. Indeed, by the time he graduates he will have earned more than 500 credits (compared to a normal high school load of 220). His internship at Willow Garage is a full work week during the summer and one day a week during the school year. In addition to work and school, Tony also builds robots, is active in his local science and robotics community, and performs pro bono work for small businesses.

Given this full load of courses, work, robot-building, and extracurricular activities, Tony has been able to successfully manage his work and time, completing tasks in a timely manner.

It has been a privilege and a pleasure to support Tony during the past years. He is one of the most able and accomplished students I've worked with during my 48 years in education. I'm certain that this able and self-motivated young man would be an outstanding student at Stanford [or other school]. I strongly recommend him with a great deal of enthusiasm and with no reservations whatsoever.

Tony's transcript consisted of three pages that showed course titles, grades, credits, and SAT scores, and another seven pages of course descriptions. Some of the course titles for his "classes" that were not at the community college or through EPGY were Programming in Python, Computational Intelligence, Robotics Internship I–IV, Rhetoric and Persuasion, Introduction to Japanese I and II, and Revolutions in World History. Here's the course description for Robotics Internship I.

Involved programming and software development for multiple mobile robot platforms. Languages and tools included Python, OpenCV, C++, C. Projects included:
- *Indoor navigation with A*-based planners*
- *Indoor mapping with SLAM*
- *Localization with AMCL for a mobile robot*
- *Development work on deliberative action planner (Teleo-Reactive Executive – T-REX) for a mobile robot (PR2) and used for AUV development at Monterey Bay Aquarium Research Institute*

Tony was accepted by Caltech, Carnegie Mellon, MIT, the Rose-Hulman Institute of Technology, Stanford, Stevens Institute of Technology, the University of Pennsylvania, Washington University in St. Louis, and Worchester Polytechnic Institute. He decided to attend Stanford. About his impending matriculation there he says, "I'm excited about the new experience and the many possibilities. I feel that I have a good background with reasonable experiences, but know it will be challenging and require me to develop new skills. I am really looking forward to meeting new people and to being exposed to new ideas and knowledge."

Tony gained a significant portion of his pre-university education at a community college. Many community colleges will allow students who are in a public or private school or homeschool to enroll concurrently in classes at the college. Policies and opportunities vary from state to state. For example, Lansing Community College in Michigan has a Dual Enrollment Program. Applicants must be beyond the eighth grade and working toward high school graduation. Separate policies govern admission of people who are 14 or 15 and those who are 16 and 17.[4]

Many four-year schools allow students who have not been admitted to enroll in their classes. At the University of Connecticut, high school students are eligible to take undergraduate courses on a not-for-credit basis.[5] These courses could be listed for credit on a homegrown high school transcript. Transcript-writing is discussed in Chapter 9.

Chapter 6
Stopping Out after University

At age seven, Laura Deming was deeply troubled when she thought about her father dying one day. As a consequence, she vowed to understand aging and work toward lengthening the human lifespan. Five years later she contacted the head of a laboratory at the University of California, San Francisco (UCSF), and presented herself so well that she was invited to visit the lab. Here's Laura's description of that visit in response to one her college application's prompts.

"It was my own personal nirvana. The atrium had a three-story-high statue of DNA, pentagons representing ribose were patterned into the carpet, even the lounge chairs looked like nucleotides. I fingered the plastic double helix that always hung on a chain around my neck. DNA was built into every fiber of this building; the architecture was certainly a kindred spirit. I'd come to this institute—named, appropriately enough, Genentech Hall—to visit a professor I'd always admired. Cynthia Kenyon was like the Feynman of biogerontology, my chosen field, and it was still hard to believe she'd let a naive 12-year-old like me drop by and tour her lab.

"So I jiggled nervously beside my dad as we clambered up the windy stairs to the third floor. But I stopped in shock when we reached the lab entrance. I'd envisioned rows of pristine steel benches, manned by industrious figures in white coats and pocket protectors; what I saw was a hodgepodge of flasks and vials crammed precariously onto shelves and occasionally rummaged through by ordinary-looking people hunched over microscopes or manhandling pipettes. My room looked spotless by comparison.

"I didn't know it then but I'd go on to spend the next couple years of my life entrenched in that cluttered, chaotic lab. I'd capsize experiments, capture genes, and do more than my fair share of pipette-pushing. But on that day, as I wandered through the lab peering at magnified nematodes and gawking at gels, all I knew was that, if this was science, I never wanted to do anything else. And it's been that way ever since."

I met Laura when she was 14. She had come to my office to ask whether her experiences as a homeschooler would be adequate to document and send to colleges. Would there be a chance that she would be admitted? It seemed clear to me that the answer was *Yes*.

Developing Laura's Transcript

We began an e-mail conversation that lasted for months. Laura sent me descriptions of her learning experiences and I kept asking questions until we had a transcript. It turned out to be 16 pages: three pages for a course list, showing credits and grades, most of which she and I assigned, and test scores; eight pages of course descriptions, which Laura wrote herself in a breezy, informal, and occasionally humorous way (one of these descriptions is in Chapter 9); and four evaluative letters, from a biology professor, the instructor of a Johns Hopkins distance learning course in American law and politics, and teachers of music and martial arts. The biology professor, who taught a course at UC Berkeley, one of the few formal courses that Laura took, described Laura as "a singularity in my teaching experience, which spans a quarter century and has engaged well over 10,000 undergraduates." The courses on Laura's transcript included independent endeavors using materials from several sources, audits of graduate-level courses at UCSF, and course credit for high test scores.

Laura submitted her applications and I sent in her transcript and various required reports. She was accepted at MIT, Caltech, UC campuses at Berkeley, Irvine, and Santa Barbara, and Harvey Mudd. She decided to matriculate at MIT. She was 14 years old.

20 Under 20 Thiel Fellowship

In the middle of her sophomore year Laura sent me this e-mail.

"How are you? I can't believe it's been so long!

"MIT is a great place for me. Thank you again for making it possible for me to be here. =)

"Classes are actually easier than I thought they'd be—not too easy, but not back-breakingly difficult either. I've decided to double major in physics and biology—I took a course on electromagnetism freshman year, and fell in love with Maxwell's equations, thus the physics aspirations.

"I'm also interested in synthetic biology. It's a growing field, one I think has a lot of potential. I spent freshman summer in a competition called iGEM, a team-based race to genetically engineer the coolest new organism possible. Our team worked to build a 'cellular touchpad'—a cell culture that would respond to certain patterns of touch by forming complex organ-like structures. We ended up doing pretty well in the final competition, which was super gratifying. =)

"I'm also thinking a lot about business, especially startups and biotech around MIT. In December, I applied for the 20 Under 20 program. Peter Thiel, Paypal founder, is going to invest $100,000 in 20 young people under 20. They will leave school for a year and go to California to use the money to either start a company or join a startup. I've passed the first round of the application, but they need all our old transcripts; would you mind sending my transcript to their application headquarters?"

In an e-mail three months later, Laura said, "About 20 Under 20—I got in! (But please keep this quiet until the end of the week—they haven't officially announced fellows yet.)"

Several weeks later the Thiel Foundation announced the Fellowship winners; because of the high quality of the applications, there were 24 of them. Laura's project is to work toward speeding up anti-aging research by commercializing it. This will change the research paradigm and make the results and products of studies available sooner. For more about Thiel Fellowships and Laura's project, go to http://www.thielfoundation.org/index.php?option=com_content&view=article&id=26.

Just a few days before I wrote this, Laura said in an e-mail, "Am very busy (but having a lot of fun!), . . . and meeting up with Thiel Fellow mentors (ever have those weeks where literally everyone you meet is smarter than you? I love those weeks)."

I responded that I had serious doubts about her characterization of the people she's meeting as smarter than her.

Chapter 7

An Indirect Path to Medical School

In June of 1999 I received this e-mail:

"Hi, my name is Cassi. I'm 15 and getting ready to enter my junior year. I live in Kentucky, in a county with only one high school. I attended this school from K-8th grade, skipped 6th, but in the beginning of my 9th grade year I decided to leave. Then I attended a classical education homeschool program for two years, where I went to school a few hours a week and did all my assignments at home. You have to be invited to come back, and because of some prior conflicts with the overly-Puritanical principal, I was not. The school in my county is approximately 1,000 people. I have a hard time getting along with the students there, and because of my class choices for the past two years I am unsure that I can pass the examination to be readmitted into the 11th grade. I finished a rigorous 98-99 school year with grades ranging from 93-99, but since I have not had geometry this creates a problem for readmission into the county school.

"My goals are to attend perhaps Johns Hopkins University and become a psychiatrist. My SAT scores are V-660 M-620. Please write me, and tell me more about your school and enrollment."

This e-mail marked the beginning of an intense, months-long conversation over a distance about how Casandra Miller would get to college. We talked about various ways to finish high school, whether or not to work toward early college admission, which colleges were attractive to her, and how financial aid works. Within a month, Casandra was seriously considering early college and began a college search. She wrote, "When I first began looking at colleges, I practically fell in love with Wells." She decided to graduate from Beach High School and we began developing a transcript. It became clear that, for practical reasons having to do with timing, it would work well to begin at a college in Kentucky and then transfer to Wells College in New York. After experiencing rude and dismissive treatment from a dean at one college, Casandra set her sights on Midway College. Both Wells and Midway are women's colleges.

Forming a Plan

When a plan grew into a complete one that looked like it would work, Casandra wrote, "I am positively ELATED! I am so happy, it seems like all this has finally pulled itself together—I have been down what seems every avenue possible and now found one that works perfectly!"

The work that Casandra had done in the classical homeschool education program went on her BHS transcript, as did three courses she completed at the county high school. She enrolled in and completed five correspondence courses with Keystone National High School. She told me about many outside-of-school activities she had participated in and we discussed grades and credits for these learning experiences. Here are some examples of the transcript entries for these activities.

Course	Grade/Credits	
Kentucky Youth Assembly, 1995, 1996, 1997	A	6

A three-day youth-in-government program sponsored by the YMCA. Over 300 bills and amendments have been passed in the Kentucky legislature that were designed and passed through this program. Casandra co-authored a bill, served in the House of Representatives, argued a case in the chambers of the state capital, and served on a committee for writing legislation during her three years of attendance. She learned much about the workings of government, and learned how to thoroughly research case studies.

Summer Camp for Academically Talented Students	A+	10

Western Kentucky University, 1995, 1996, 1997
A two-week residential program, sponsored by the Center for Gifted Students. During her three years of attending, Casandra studied a variety of subjects in studio arts, American history, science, and drama.

Travel to Japan	A+	13

Work Skills	A+	20

Through her jobs at Subway and Steak 'n Shake, Casandra learned to use and increase her strong work ethic, the basics of commerce, fast food preparation and sanitation, money/register skills, customer service, and good business etiquette. She gained in strength and coordination.

Volunteer Work	B	3

At Jeffersontown branch of the Louisville Free Public Library.

Academic Skills	A	6

SAT I, 1/97: V - 610, M - 520; SAT I, 6/99: V - 660, M – 620
ACT, 10/99: English - 30; Mathematics - 25; Reading - 32; Science Reasoning - 29; Composite – 29

Credits are according to the California scheme of 10 credits per year-long course. My belief is that credits should be awarded for what's learned and its value, not for time spent. A year's worth of credit is for the amount of learning in a typical year-long high school course. I don't believe it's actually possible to accurately measure an "amount of learning," but there's a game to be played in working toward college admission.

Because Casandra needed a diploma to enter Midway College before she had completed some high school coursework, three of her courses at Keystone and one (the only one) at Beach High School were listed on her transcript as post-high-school work completed after her date of graduation. Her BHS course was English 4: Literature, Composition, & Critical Thinking. Credit for this course was based on book reviews and essays that Casandra had sent me, and on the critical thinking she had done throughout our work together.

Determination, Will, and Perseverance

Casandra completed a semester at Midway, transferred to Wells, where she was on the Dean's List for four of her six semesters, and graduated magna cum laude at 19 with a major in psychology and a minor in music. She was awarded the Margaret Schwartz Psychology Prize (shared) and Distinction in the major field of Psychology. She returned to Kentucky, and during the next two years she worked and completed some medical school prerequisites at the University of Kentucky. Her work was varied; it included teaching ESL to Japanese speakers, serving as a mental health associate in an outpatient psychiatric facility, and working as a pharmacy technician. She applied and was admitted to the University of Louisville School of Medicine.

During the summer of 2006, on my way to visit Brian (see Chapter 1) in Indiana, I flew to Louisville to meet Casandra in person for the first time, seven years after I began working with her. We found that conversation was very easy, and talked for six hours one afternoon and another two the next morning before I made my way to Indiana.

Since then we have spent time together on two other occasions, once at my home in California and once at her home in Florida, where she was (and as I write this, still is) a resident in family medicine at a medical center there. A close working relationship has grown into a close friendship, maintained mostly through e-mail.

Casandra married while she was in medical school; she and her husband have welcomed their first child.

She struggled at times with her science and math classes. While taking me on a driving tour of Louisville during my visit there, she talked of some difficult times in medical school. I foolishly asked her if she would make it through. Without hesitation she said, "Of course." In a letter recommending Casandra for high school graduation, her mother wrote, "I feel that Casandra's strengths lie in her determination, will, and perseverance." It is my belief that these personal traits are the underlying reasons for Casandra's successes in college and medical school, and the fundamental reasons why she is a very good doctor.

Chapter 8

Other Less-Traveled Paths

I've written about some of the former students I've known best and kept in touch with. Their education and work have been largely in scientific or technical fields; however, it is not the case that most of my students have chosen to work in these areas. Many of them have found their passions and vocations in the arts, humanities, sports, crafts, and business.

Three former students, all of whom graduated from BHS at 15, left formal academic education behind and went on to enlarge talents that were already well developed. One is now a principal dancer with a big-city ballet company, another is a successful singer and recording artist, and yet another is a professional rock climber.

The Irish Musician

In 1995 I wrote about Theo Paige in a newsletter I was then publishing:

Theo Paige took the California High School Proficiency Examination in April of 1994 and failed it. Recognizing that the exam in no way measured his real intelligence and talents, he submitted as his application for a BHS diploma a wonderful essay and a tape of the music he creates. I liked the essay so much that I immediately made it the sample essay in the packet I give to people explaining how they can earn a diploma. Theo's diploma was his ticket into Cabrillo College; last May, at age 16, he finished his first full year as a college student, completing a number of courses in several fields and earning solid grades.

In the 1997 edition of the same newsletter, I wrote:

. . . [Theo Paige] has recorded a CD; he plays fiddle, guitar, bodhrán, and harmonica and is accompanied by several other people in this production of Irish reels, jigs, and airs. The album is titled simply Theo Paige. Theo is now immersing himself in his music; he is planning travel to Europe, attendance at music school, and an apprenticeship.

When this chapter was nearly finished, I went for a walk and happened to encounter Theo, whom I had not seen or heard from for many years. He told me that music is still at the center of his life and that he had just returned from a three-year stay in Ireland. In a subsequent e-mail he wrote:

"When I was a kid I was not interested in being pressured and softened up by a high school curriculum that aimed me away from my special interests and talents, which I wanted to develop over time. This was for me things like violin, self education, and art. I like to explore the attitudes of ancient times and compare them to now. In my music, this revives my skills and opens the door to new expressions.

"I was last in high school 17 years ago. Since then I have had a steady home life and have been abroad, where I spent the past few years putting my talents to good use in Ireland, where gigs pay decently for me. I won the Midwest Comhaltas Ceoltoiri Na hErin competition last year. This year I won second place, and also first place with my [two] friends on flute and banjo in the group category. I've kept my life eventful and meditative and made a druid friend who showed me around the ancient ruins in Ireland. The idea of advancing as a human, and not just a musician, appeals to me the most—to be always at the mercy of the Golden Rule."

The Novelist

I also learned of Grace Krilanovich's career as I was writing this book:

"I left high school early to start college, at age 17, in 1996. After two AA degrees from Cabrillo College, I went on to get a Bachelors in American studies from San Francisco State University and a Masters of Fine Arts at California Institute of the Arts (CalArts) in writing. Today, I work at the *Los Angeles Times*, but my main career focus is as a writer of fiction.

"Last year my debut novel, *The Orange Eats Creeps*, was published; it is now in its third printing. I started writing the novel during grad school and then finished it in early 2007. It took almost three years to find a publisher, but in the end I was thrilled when Two Dollar Radio, a small press out of Ohio, published it in September of 2010. Since then it's been successful beyond my wildest imaginings, making best of the year lists at NPR, BlackBook, and *Shelf Unbound Magazine*, and was one of Amazon's Top 10 Science Fiction/Fantasy books of 2010. Last November, I was deeply honored to be named one of the National Book Foundation's "5 Under 35" for 2010.

"Now I'm at work on a second novel. An excerpt of that was published this spring in the lit journal, *Puerto del Sol*. I also have various nonfiction pieces, book and film reviews, etc. forthcoming or recently published, mostly in online mags."

Personal Reflections

My own experiences in schools led me to the work I'm now doing. I spent four empty years in high school, drifting along without paying much attention or learning a lot, and getting, with one exception, all A's. I went directly to UCLA and was shocked at the high level at which I was expected to perform. I learned to adapt, but my undergraduate education would have meant much more to me if I had had some earlier life experience outside of schools. During a year that included my 49th birthday, I earned an M.A. in educational counseling, and that turned out to be, like high school, a mostly empty experience.

My 32 years working in public and private schools taught me how the traditional system works, how it fails to support and nurture some kids, and how to outmaneuver it. EAE, my program for gifted students at Middleroad High School, provided an apprenticeship for my present work. A great deal of what I've learned as the director of Beach High School, I learned in an unschooling way.

I derive enormous pleasure from supporting young people in avoiding inappropriate traditional schooling and finding education that is truly fulfilling.

Chapter 9

Writing Transcripts

In California and more than a dozen other states, state laws allow homeschooling families to set up their own private schools. Beach High School was established and is maintained under these same laws. I can do everything that any other school can do in spite of the fact that I have no classrooms, athletic fields, or teachers. Your state's laws may similarly allow you to direct your own school. (Please check with your local homeschool association or network for more information.)

If you are in a state where you cannot set up a school, you can nevertheless write a transcript to supplement or use in place of a traditional school transcript. On a transcript, you can document all learning regardless of how it was acquired or where it took place.

I wrote transcripts for Jerimi (Chapter 3), Tony (Chapter 5), Laura (Chapter 6), and Casandra (Chapter 7) that were part of their successful applications to four-year colleges. Here are some guidelines to follow if you write a transcript for your daughter or son.

There is no universally-expected format for a high school transcript.

Design a format that best presents, in an easy-to-understand way, the abilities and accomplishments of the person it represents. Do not use a template unless you cannot think of a better way to show the information that needs to be shown. If a transcript is very long, show a summary up front and follow with details, like course descriptions, evaluative letters, etc.

The amount of detail included on a transcript depends on how much outside evaluation can be provided.

If most academic work has been done officially at recognized institutions, little detail is required. If most work has been done independently without institutional credit having been given, a great deal of detail should be included; a simple list of courses, grades, and credits will not do the job. Any or all of the following elements can be included when a detailed transcript is needed.

Heading

This can include the name and location of your school and the student's name, address, phone number, date of birth, parent(s)'s name(s), date of enrollment, and graduation date.

Course List

This list can include course titles, grades, credits, and possibly brief pieces of narrative. Course titles should be as descriptive as possible, while also being brief; for example, list "U.S. History–WWII to the Present" rather than simply "History." If courses have been taken at various places, include a key explaining indicative symbols included with course titles. Courses can be listed chronologically or by subject, and as year, semester, or quarter courses. I don't think it's possible to accurately describe and measure anyone's learning or achievement with numbers and letters of the alphabet, so don't worry about being exact or comparing what your son or daughter has done with what others do in high school. Just assign grades and credits that make sense to you. In California, most high schools award 10 credits for a typical year's work; in many other states, it's 1 credit for a year course. If something has been of greater value than usual, you can assign more credits, fractional if necessary. You can also assign fewer. Courses can be designated as honors courses when levels of achievement warrant it.

Here's a short section of a course list.

Course	Grade/Credit	
Ninth Grade		
American Literature (LAF, PD)	**A+**	**10.0**
Introduction to the PC	**A+**	**2.5**
Course at Pelican County College		
General Invertebrate Biology (SD)	**A**	**5.0**
With field work		

This list was preceded by a key, showing, for example, that SD stands for "self-designed coursework."

Credits and GPA

Provide a total number of credits and a grade point average (GPA). An A is worth 4 grade points, a B 3, and so on. Honors courses get an extra grade point. Here's a simple example of a GPA computation.

1 A in an honors course:	1 grade x 5 grade points =	5.0 grade points
3 A's:	3 x 4 =	12.0
1 A-:	1 x 3.7 =	3.7
2 B's:	2 x 3 =	6.0
Grade point total:		26.7

Grade points divided by number of grades = 26.7 / 7 = **3.81 = GPA**

Narratives

Use narratives of any length wherever necessary to provide clear explanations of your kid's home education. Explanations can be a description of your homeschooling philosophy and methods, a piece written by your son or daughter, course descriptions, etc. For example:

The Pelican County Co-op is a support network of homeschooling parents. We are from Brownville, Greenburg, Red Hill, Black City, and surrounding areas. We share our talents and energies in a co-operative environment. PCC meets regularly for the purpose of providing enjoyable, creative, and educational activities so our children can celebrate the adventures of learning and explore their world together. . . . A wide variety of co-op groups—book discussion clubs, for example—are organized for children of all ages to share and explore in such subjects as literature, history, math, and science.

Course Descriptions

Course descriptions should include content, methods, and materials used. Laura wrote all her course descriptions; here's an example.

Calculus with analytic geometry, *3/07–7/07: After I worked through the Saxon calculus book, I got the textbook MIT uses for their calculus courses,* Calculus with Analytic Geometry *(Simmons), and started working problems from it. These problems were much more complex and required creative thinking; sometimes a problem would take days to solve. It was like a crash course for my calculus skills. I also did part of the MIT textbook for multivariable calculus,* Multivariable Calculus *(Edwards & Penney)*

Reading Lists

You can include a comprehensive list or separate lists for different subject areas.

Letters of Evaluation/Recommendation

Entire letters and/or excerpts can be used. A short excerpt might be included as part of a course description, a course listing might include a note that says "See attached evaluation," or a more general letter can simply be added to a transcript.

Other Documentation

Include anything that adds to the description and evaluation of your kid's learning. For example, if he or she has worked with a substantial number of other people, you could include a list of teachers and mentors showing titles and qualifications.

Length

I've written transcripts that are 15 or more pages in length. They have typically presented a course list up front, followed by whatever other detailed material we deemed necessary.

Chapter 10

Taking Control

One day at Middleroad High School, Tierney Wayne, who was in her junior year, came to my classroom to talk about taking the California High School Proficiency Examination (CHSPE), which did not require that she have any school official's permission to take, and which, if she passed, would give her a Certificate of Proficiency, a high-school-diploma-equivalent certificate that would allow her to follow her plan to leave high school and enter a community college. Her mother, a single parent who taught in a public elementary school, approved.

With this plan in place, Tierney decided that she didn't want to continue with one of her six high school classes. This became a big issue; school administrators didn't want to let her drop the class. A before-school meeting was set up to discuss the issue, with Tierney, her mother, the school principal, Tierney's counselor, and me scheduled to attend.

The school would lose no funding if Tierney dropped a class. There were many junior students who had been dropped from classes by the school because they had been cutting. No one argued that Tierney needed to learn the material in the class in question, and no one doubted that she would pass the CHSPE. But her request to drop was denied on the grounds that there was a rule—that juniors were required to take six classes. The purpose of the rule was to keep students on track toward graduation—but Tierney, with her mother's support, had decided not to graduate, a decision that was hers to make.

Middleroad's principal wouldn't allow Tierney to make a decision about dropping a class, but Tierney still took control of the life she would lead after high school. She took the CHSPE, passed it, left high school, compiled a strong record at a community college, transferred to San Jose State University, and earned a degree in molecular biology. She has had a position at the Stanford Genome Center, and is now a research engineer employed by the University of Texas, working in a lab doing "a little sequencing, some real-time PCR, a lot of genotyping." (PCR, polymerase chain reaction, enables researchers to produce millions of copies of a specific DNA sequence in a short period of time.) She is an author on seven scientific papers. She didn't need her school counselor or principal to figure out how to pursue her education or live her life.

Who has the Power?

Compulsory education is based on compulsion. Compulsion requires power over students and control of them. Power and control often become the chief concerns.

School officials were in a position of power from which they could control Tierney's life in school as long as she was enrolled. They thought they should exercise their control to be sure that everyone, including Tierney, regardless of differences in interests, strengths, talents, and goals, should passively accept what they wanted to deliver. They were incapable of understanding, or unwilling to acknowledge that they understood, the fact that there are many perfectly legitimate and real reasons why some kids hate school.

Many students find no challenging material to study; they are capable of working at a much higher level than the curriculum allows. Their interests are not addressed; the academic curriculum in traditional high schools has little to offer someone who wants to be, or already is, a photographer, dancer, auto mechanic, or makeup artist. They do not like the social environment; they want to talk about topics beyond the latest clothing fad or the next party, football game, or sexual encounter. They find their teachers disinterested and sometimes incompetent. They find the environment oppressive and limiting, determining not only what they study but also when they can go to the bathroom or chew gum. They hate being controlled at every turn. They don't like being on leashes held by administrators, counselors, and teachers. They resent it when their talents and goals are not respected. While this kind of rigid structure may work well for some students, this determination should still be made by the student with his or her parents.

Grabbing the Reins

To provide your child with a fitting and fulfilling education, you may need to take control. In Chapter 1, I said that you may need to investigate carefully, dig deep, and persist in seeking information about community college admission. Finding other information may also require patience and persistence.

One day at Middleroad High School, a student came to talk to me about what her counselor had told her about the California High School Proficiency Exam (CHSPE). It was all wrong. I decided to call other high schools to see if accurate information was readily available elsewhere.

I called ten high schools in an adjacent county, talked with people ranging from secretaries to vice principals, and asked the same two questions in each conversations: *Who is eligible to take the CHSPE? Is the certificate earned through the exam acceptable to the University of California?* The facts were (and are) that a person was eligible to take the CHSPE if s/he was 16 on the day of the test, if s/he had completed a year of the 10th grade, or if s/he was in the second semester of the 10th grade. The University of California (UC) had for years before I made these calls stated in its basic literature that the Certificate of Proficiency earned through the CHSPE was acceptable in lieu of a regular diploma. It still is.

Not one of the calls I made yielded correct answers to both questions. One vice principal told me that he was proud that no student at his school had ever taken "that thing," a term that he almost spat into the phone. I was told several times that a student could take the exam when he was a certain age, but this age varied, and I was not told of the other eligibility criteria; a student who had skipped a grade or two would be eligible at an age younger than 16. Several people told me that UC would not accept the certificate.

A few years later I continued this experiment and called five more high schools. The fifth one answered both questions correctly. One out of fifteen is 7 percent, a failing grade on any grading scale.

The best way to obtain accurate information is to get as close to the source as you can. In the case of the CHSPE, the source is their online information bulletin (at http://chspe.net/), not high school counselors, neighbors, or people on e-lists. The source for information about college admissions is at college admissions offices. Unfortunately, sometimes conflicting, confusing, or erroneous information will come even from people whom you'd expect to be experts.

Recently a mom called me, disturbed because she and her daughter had been told by a UC representative that a high school diploma was required for junior-level transfer applicants at her UC campus. For years the policy at all UC campuses had not required a diploma. I called the university's admissions office and was told that a diploma was required. Still not believing it, I e-mailed the dean of admissions. She sent my query to another person, who replied this way:

Submission of a high school record is required of all junior transfer students, assuming that high school work was completed and a diploma, GED or California High School Proficiency Exam was received. A junior transfer student should not retroactively obtain high school graduation equivalency for UC admission. Students should clearly indicate in their application high school attendance and any diploma or certificate received. They should also explain their individual circumstances that might affect what records may or may not be available. Eligibility as a junior transfer is not affected but the information and records are needed to complete a student's educational history.

And so, after being misinformed several times and working through some verbiage, we learned that the long-term policy is still in force and that a high school diploma is not required.

When you need information, look carefully, talk to many people, read widely, check and double check. But don't wait to act until you've reached complete certainty, or you'll get permanently stuck.

During the time that Brian (Chapter 1) audited community college classes, college policy did not allow auditing, but a vice president of the college allowed it anyway. After you've gathered as much information as you think you need and find that what you want is not permissible, you can still seek special permission from people in appropriate positions.

As I hope I've made clear, established schools and traditional programs may fall short of providing your daughter or son with an enjoyable, appropriate, and fulfilling education. Keep in mind that forging a new path may lead to interesting and exciting opportunities that traditional education simply cannot provide. You may need to take control. Don't fear the challenge, embrace it.

Appendix A

Photos

To give an even more personal feel to the stories contained in this book, I've included photos of the people whose educational paths I discussed. I hope the stories have helped you realize that anyone with determination, perseverance, and will can forge his or her own educational path.

Brian Beach
Chapter 1, From No High School to Graduate School
Photo Credit: U.U.C.C.I.

Matthew Snyder
Chapter 2, A Short Stay in Public High School Leads to Graduate School, Eventually
Photo Credit: Karla Galdamez

Jerimi Walker
Chapter 3, Autodidact Finds a Way to Soar
Photo Credit: Jerimi Walker

Ciera Kash
Chapter 4, "Real World" Success Without College
Photo Credit: Wes Beach

Tony Pratkanis
Chapter 5, Straight from Homeschool to University
Photo Credit: Tony Pratkanis

Laura Deming
Chapter 6, Stopping Out after University
Photo Credit: Christopher Rasch

Casandra Miller
Chapter 7, An Indirect Path to Medical School
Photo Credit: Donal C.

Theo Paige
Chapter 8, Other Less-Traveled Roads: The Irish Musician
Photo Credit: Theo Paige

Grace Krilanovich
Chapter 8, Other Less-Traveled Roads: The Novelist
Photo Credit: Scott Tarasco

Resources

Your best resources are your determination, persistence, and creativity in finding the schools, programs, organizations, people, books, websites, and other supports that will be useful in creating an educational path for your kid. Here are a few books and websites that I have found informative and stimulating.

Books

The Childhood Roots of Adult Happiness: Five Steps to Help Kids Create and Sustain Lifelong Joy, by Edward M. Hallowell.

Doing School: How We Are Creating a Generation of Stressed-Out, Materialistic, and Miseducated Students, by Denise Clark Pope.

Genius Denied: How to Stop Wasting Our Brightest Young Minds, by Jan Davidson, Bob Davidson, and Laura Vanderkam.

Making the Choice: When Typical School Doesn't Fit Your Atypical Child, by Corin Barsily Goodwin and Mika Gustavson, MFT.

The Talent Code: Greatness Isn't Born, It's Grown. Here's How., by Daniel Coyle. (Note: I don't agree entirely with the premise of the title, but this is thought-provoking reading.)

Websites

Blake Boles' Zero Tuition College
    http://www.ztcollege.com

Davidson Institute for Talent Development, especially the articles provided at:
    http://www.davidsongifted.org/db/browse_by_topic_articles.aspx

The Gifted Homeschoolers Forum
    http://giftedhomeschoolers.org/

Peter Gray's blog, especially the piece at:
    http://www.psychologytoday.com/blog/freedom-
    learn/201108/is-real-educational-reform-possible-if-so-how

Hoagies' Gifted Education Page
    http://www.hoagiesgifted.org/

Homefires–The Journal of Homeschooling Online
    http://www.homefires.com/

Homeschooling A to Z
    http://homeschooling.gomilpitas.com/

Endnotes

[1]http://www.azleg.state.az.us/FormatDocument.asp?inDoc=/ars/15/01821.htm&Title=15&DocType=ARS

[2]http://www.tcc.edu/students/admissions/adm_special.htm

[3]http://admissions.uoregon.edu/transfer#transferrequirements

[4]http://www.lcc.edu/admissions/dual/

[5]http://continuingstudies.uconn.edu/nondegree/ndstudy.html

About the Author

Wes Beach worked in public schools for 31 years, mostly in high schools, and in a private school for one year. He taught science, math, and English, and directed programs for gifted and "at-risk" kids. He wised up in 1993, left the system, and has since then directed Beach High School, which consists of a home office and an attitude–the attitude expressed in this book. He is at present the Teen Adviser for both the Gifted Homeschoolers Forum (GHF) and the HomeSchool Association of California (HSC); he served on HSC's board for two years. He has spoken at many conferences (especially at HSC's in Sacramento each year), written a number of articles, and authored another book, *Opportunities After High School: Thoughts, Documents, Resources.* He is an outside consultant for the Davidson Institute for Talent Development, and in 2005 received a Distinguished Service Award from the California Association for the Gifted. For more articles by Wes, please check out the Articles page at www.giftedhomeschoolers.org.

(Photo credit: Nalina Clark)

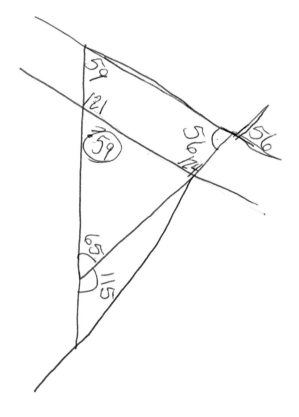

Made in the USA
Lexington, KY
11 January 2012